Laugh Lines, Tear Stains

Jemima Woods

BookLeaf Publishing

India | USA | UK

Presentation by *BookLeaf Publishing*

Web: www.bookleafpub.com

E-mail: info@bookleafpub.com

ISBN: 9789358317008

First edition 2024

For Berry

PREFACE

I've always loved connecting with people. I'm that person who smiles at you through the driver's side window whilst sitting at a set of traffic lights or drunkenly tells you, "I love your earrings!" in the smoking area of a nightclub (even though I don't smoke).

I've always loved to tell stories and found an overwhelming number of ways to connect with people by doing so. Whether it's being vulnerable or telling a thigh-slapper, storytelling is within each of us. Poetry can be such a romantic, devastating and stupidly amusing way of storytelling, and with many different styles each poet shares, you're bound to relate at some point, in one way or another. Whether it's positive four-liners from Lemn Sissay's 'Let the Light Pour In' or it's hopeful romance from Celia Martinez or it's like mine, a mixture of inspiration from Sissay and Martinez, life and people in general. Whoever you are and whatever you like, there's something here for you. To laugh, love, grieve or appreciate is to live, and as an artist, you are taught to find inspiration in everything; I'd like to say my poetry reflects that. So, this book is not only for you; it's from you.

It's from and for my beautiful friends, Gabija, Isobel and Renata. It's from and for my incredibly supportive family. It's from and for my beloved Cocker Spaniel 'Berry' who sadly passed away this year. It's from and for my tutors at university, especially Krissi, who gave me a chance when it felt like no one else would. It's *really* from and for the wasp that flew into my face at 7 am that prompted me to write 'Monday's'.

But finally, It's for you, from me.

Enjoy.

Table of Contents

Poems for a Smile & the Downright Daft

Introduction

I wrote a poem for you
Yes you
You with those… eyes.

Good job, keep it vague so that everyone can
relate. Nice.

Yes, you with those eyes
Reading each word as if they were written for
someone else
Someone… not you.
But this poem
This poem
Is for you

It's everything you need to hear, even if I don't
say it
Or write it
Rather

It's whatever you want it to be
It's funny
Witty
Clever

Cheeky
Heartfelt
Truthful, the good kind
Or the harsh kind, whichever you prefer

Look, I'm sorry, I know you expected it to be
better
But we have only just met
And this might not be the best poem you've ever
read
But at least you can say it's yours
Yeah you
With those eyes
Or
Eye

^Just on the off chance a pirate is reading this.

Monday's

I killed a man today, in cold blood
I was minding my business, early in the morn
I sat innocently by the fountain, watching
squirrels dancing around searching for acorns
I didn't see the man, until I killed him of course
I was actually quite enjoying my morning, until I
traumatised him with blunt force
I thought I was safe here
Before him, nature and I had a special bond
I suppose I won't get that back now, after I
kicked his body into the pond.
He had a buzz cut and a puffer jacket
It was self-defence
That's what I will say if anyone asks
Danger flashed before my eyes; I literally saw
yellow and black
I was hit, square in the face
And upon gracing my skin, he fell to the floor
soon after
So, I stood on his head and yelled
"'Av that ya b*stard!"

I don't like wasps. Especially when they fly into
my face at 7 am.

Technical Turbulence

One ear quieter than the other
Supporting music through one
Blaring lyrics through another

I hoped they would work
As I plugged them into my phone
They sort of do
But only through one ear though
The first song I put on
Was really sad
Oh how fitting in theme
As my headphones only half-work now
After going through the washing machine

Goodness Gracious

Trying to loosen my collar
Sweat dripping from my head
"It's bloody scorching in this car!"
I frustratedly said

My back is on fire
"It's twenty-six degrees outside!"
"Can we at least open a window?"
I desperately cried

Uncomfortably wriggling
Accompanied by mischievous sniggering
Searching, frantically, for the source of the
added heat one sunny afternoon
I discovered my heated seat had been turned on,
in the middle of June...

Zeus the God-Dog Who's Scared of Plates

He's got a fluffy head and one dodgy eye
"Scared of plates?" you asked, confused
Myself, I'm not exactly sure why

Though he was not born to the Titans
And he doesn't harness the power of lightning
He does, however
Find dish sets quite frightening

His name is Zeus, but by no means is he a god
He most resembles his beard
Because our Zeus is a dog

A god that is quite cowardly
Oh doesn't that sound absurd
Ironic if I tell you Zeus is also afraid of birds

Falling objects
Loud noises
Shadows
And doors
Will surely make this god-dog scurry on all
fours

Sexual infidelity is known as Zeus' biggest flaw
But to our Zeus, there is no greater scandal
Than the opening of the front door

So yes, he does have a fluffy head and one
dodgy eye
If you ask me, "Scared of plates?"
I'll tell you I'm not exactly sure why

Though he was not born to the Titans
And he does not harness the power of lightning
Unlike the courage in the history of his name
Zeus finds quite nearly everything, at least a
little bit frightening

Rice Krispies

My mum once had a hangover from hell
It was as you can imagine
Sunglasses on and curtains shut
She asked me quietly
Can you make me some cereal, please?
So I went downstairs and I made her a bowl of
Rice Krispies
I paired it with a spoon, then she asked me, "Can
I have a glass of water too?"
I chose Rice Krispies
Because I loved
The way that they would
Snap
Crackle
And pop
But upon my return
I found my mum leaning over the bowl
Quietly whispering to them
"Shut the f*ck up"

Innuendo

I once met a man named Gianfranco

No, I've not made that up

Nice man, met him through a friend, himself
also a friend, to my friend's family, at an event
my friend and I performed at, hosted by my
friend's family, in which Gianfranco is, in fact, a
friend of. His wife, Rachel, I met too, a lovely
woman and a friend of my friend's family, she
was, and well, still is, and Gianfranco too.

Undeniably, Gianfranco is a very funny man

Extremely interested in the arts, he asked my
friend and I about the process as a team, the
process of the show that my friend and I
performed at an event hosted by my friend's
family, in which Gianfranco and Rachel, his
wife, are friends of.

Not to mention his suggestions for some titles of
shows we could make, which included (but
not limited to) 'I'm going to f*** you h*rd: A
show about Brexit'

Don't get me wrong, they weren't bad at all

Only it seemed like every show had something
to do with innuendos

Mother Moon

She looks so perfect, how stunningly dressed
Like a groom on his wedding day, I look at the
white and feel blessed
Illuminating the ground around me, she shines
so bright
Like a teen with a crush, thoughts of her keep
me awake at night

For her to be seen
The sun will rise, only to fall to his knees
Their relationship replicated throughout nature
For there are no flowers without bees
There are no plants without seeds
There is no shade without trees
And the apple simply wouldn't fall, without
gravity

She is just so admired, watched in each phase
Referenced in love and I feel beautiful in her
gaze
With each night, she appears
Different in size, curved in shape
Like a thoughtful insomniac, I can't help but
stay awake

She is my only one, but I have seen another before
Do you think Mars feels lucky, that she has two versions of her to adore
And Saturn has hundreds more
But I don't care about those, because she is ours
And Earth's love for her burns deep, in her core

Sundays

I have a love-hate relationship with Sundays
I don't always have something to do
I like to cook
Motown blaring out my speaker
I like to imagine what I'll be like when I'm older

I want to be a friendly neighbour
One who will take care of your plants whilst
you're on holiday
I want to be the type of person that makes too
many cookies and then delivers them to people I
love for the rest of the day
I want to have game nights
I want to have my own traditions
I want to dance around my kitchen
And sing my own awful Motown renditions
But most of all
I want to enjoy every Sunday
Even if I don't always have something to do.

Pesaro

Pesaro is your new home for a while
She owns a fountain of seahorses I hope make
you smile
You are close to the sea
For which I am glad
As I have always watched you admire it
Feet buried deep in sand

Venice held you for just a moment
And a pizza with olives captured you in your
stride
Exploring different places
And drinking Italian wine

As you collect your stamps for places you've
flown
We hold a special place for you
A place you can always call home
Because watching you reach a dream, fills my
whole heart
Reminding me that no matter the distance
True friends are never really apart

For Old Times' Sake

Within footpaths trodden by memories, we roam
A giggle that echos, our past selves we've outgrown
For old times' sake, we turn the key
Unlocking memories, now treasured to me

The dusty attic of time unfolds,
Within each floorboard, a story it holds
Photographs and cards we used to make
Folded and faded, Nan's recipe of a banana cake
Pick out the ingredients, lay them out ready to make
How your heart can heal, doing things for old times' sake

Nostalgic embrace; it's a gentle calm
In quieter moments, a golden charm
A drink in the pub, maybe two or three
A slap of the thigh, or maybe the knee
Reminiscing on how life used to be

Take a walk around the place we once grew
Or play Monopoly all afternoon
Sit on the baseball field and enjoy the view
It doesn't matter if we're late

When we're older, we'll waste time on our
college break
How your heart can heal, doing things for old
times' sake

A glass of whiskey on Christmas Day,
Carters' pool cue in hand, ready to play
A ticket of use anywhere in Merseyside,
Saveaway
Like a scratch card, scratch away and mark your
day
The salt air by the sea keeps a cold at bay

A peach each on an open-top bus
Sandwiches packed full of jam, no crusts
Laughing with your sister
A nostalgic feeling you cannot shake
How your heart can heal, doing things for old
times' sake

Sunsets glowing, skies filled with hues of
apricot and pink
Reflect on the waters by where we used to think
For old times' sake, we raise a toast
To the memories we've made and the people we
love most

Throughout the night, stars lay awake

Guarding our stories and the relationships we
make
For old times' sake, no matter how big we grow
We revisit our pasts, in the places we know

So let us wander, hand in hand
Through the forests of what we understand
For old times' sake, when it all seems to fade
We'll forever find peace in the memories we've
made

Reliving memories, in the most meaningful of
ways
"For old times' sake"
What a wonderful phrase

Where's your Happy Place?

Does it have water?
Does it lie peacefully beside a stream?
Does it have seagulls fighting over chips?
Does it have sand by the sea?

Or is it a designated bench?
Does it sit beside a tree?
The one you will always go to
Accompanied by iced coffee

Or is it a waterfall?
A peaceful roar of nature
A place not many people know about
But a place you could sit forever

Or can it be a person?
Does it have to be a place?
Does it have to be locational?
Or can it simply be a warm embrace?

For mine you must travel
More than just a mile
But it's always worth the effort
To just sit and think for a while

However different each may seem
You can still call it your space
But be sure to tell me one thing though
Where is *your* "Happy Place"?

My Doggy

My doggy solved world hunger
My doggy solved world peace
My doggy will tell you the secret, he said
If you just give him some treats

My doggy keeps his secret
He will not tell a soul
But I bet he could be persuaded
With some chicken inside his bowl

My doggy he is smart
There are no flies on him
Apart from just the one time
He got his head stuck in the bin

My doggy then reminded me
That he had leverage, of course
That I could be the hero
But he held the key within his paws

So I gave my doggy some chicken
My doggy had more than one treat
I took him on a walk
And let him chase a squirrel up a tree

My doggy used the information
And made the pamper last a week
But how foolish of me to believe him
When my doggy can't even speak

Sunglasses

Where did I put–
I could've sworn I left them on my bed...
This is a joke. HAS ANYONE SEEN MY–
Never mind... They're on my head

Poems for Thought

You know, I know

It's a silent one you see
The battle lost straight ahead
Pupils go wide and cheeks go red
The moment when nothing is heard
But everything is said

Day Thirteen

I drove past a woman the other day
I was on my way to the shops
It was raining
She was stood outside the infirmary wearing all
black
Black jumper
Black joggers too
I didn't see her shoes
Her hair was short but wavy
I remember thinking I liked it

Something about her caught my attention and
our eyes locked for just a moment as I drove
past
I wondered why she stood out there and why of
all people she had locked eyes with me
She looked sad
Not the kind of crying sad
A deeper sadness
One that goes beyond the surface
I could see it behind her eyes
Like not only her heart was in pain
Her soul was too
The kind of sadness that eats away at your
stomach

I felt it for a moment too

I felt like I knew her
Or I should know her
I knew nothing about her
But I did know she was hurting
And I hope that she is okay
That one day she is happier and isn't feeling so
blue
And if I do see her again
I hope her shoes aren't black too

Hands

The problem with loving some men
Is they will often have big hands
Great for capturing an opinion
Or enforcing one's demands

But our love, it turns to liquid
We drip through the cracks in their fingers
They promise to collect the drops
And then we forget the cracks existed

But we must've fallen through something
To seep so deep within the ground
Only to be mopped up later
Holding the illusion of being found

We don't know how to be grateful for those
hands
When they hold so much more than our voice
Then we're haunted by the reminder
That loving them is our choice

Force of Habit

The voicemail they made together now rings, familiar songs
Avoiding places claimed by him, places he belongs
On the kitchen side she places two cups, a routine of love that only loss disrupts
Only now she pours for one, force of habit still unwon
The flowers go feral without the garden manager to run
She's useless at that stuff, he was the one with the green thumb
She forgets to lock the door and turn off the light
Since he was the one to run around at night
She still irons his shirts, folding them neatly in a pile
She fixes her hair in the mirror, but no longer in the reflection is his adoring smile
Each anniversary a reminder of what once was
No more flowers on a random Sunday "just because"
But still she sticks to her routine
Force of habit she will blame
One day their house will be known as a place they were both once seen

And his heart she will seek to reclaim

29

Well..?

When the darkness lingers
Do you welcome it with comforting arms?
Or do you point at it
With accusing fingers?

The Straw

I used to be very angry
Sometimes, sit frustratedly crying
But there soon comes a day
You. Just. Stop. Trying.

Berry

What do you do
With a bowl big enough for two
When
One of them is gone

Oh how your heart will ache
Calling for man's best mate
When you realise
The trots of paws
Now echo in fours
And no longer in eights

Poems from a Hopeful Romantic

Love Language

A shared language of two hearts that connect
Loving, sweet and devoted to protect
In quiet glances
Or a touch that lingers
Expressed proudly
Or through a squeeze of intertwined fingers

Written in verses or in words unsaid
My love cooks breakfast and cuts a heart shape
into the bread
In grand gestures, love takes flight
Whilst quiet whispers of devotion, linger on in
the night

In compromises made, in thoughtful deeds done
proudly
Love shouts from the rooftops, declaring fate
loudly
In laughs shared and in sorrow we hold
Love is in gestures made tender and bold

So whether you whisper or fearlessly declare
Love's aura is felt because it's a tenderness we
share

Each language of confessing, love is proudly
shown
Unique in their entirety, each speaking their own

'Everything' Bagel

She parked her car quite neatly between the
lines, checking the handle after it locked
A car sped past her to get out of the lot quickly,
her love tugged at her jumper harshly
A hand placed on her chest
The other by her side
As she sighed a relieved sigh, she gazed up at
his eyes
And uttered so innocently, you practically saved
my life

As she talks, he looks solely in her direction
His attention unnoticed as she ranted to the sky
He did not interrupt or counter her opinion, he
walked and listened
Never leaving her side
They entered the building and his arm rested on
her lower back
Something about their demeanour showed me,
they felt safe like that
They walked in unison, swaying side by side
Something told me that their hearts would travel
across universes to collide

A few minutes later they returned, he holding a
singular bag of bagels
They swayed in his hand as he walked
As if he was proud of his trip out with his girl
How beautiful, I thought
As I witnessed a short snippet of their life
Who knew I would encounter a love story
On a random Thursday night.

Muse

If you were my muse and I, a painter
I'd paint a garden
Bursting with bright colourful flowers
Through it butterflies would twirl and whirl with
each spin finding something new to explore
Dodging bees busily rushing around, finding the
perfect pollen spot

If you were my muse and I, a choreographer
I would make a duet
One person would play the free, the sun and the
fire
The other would play the disciplined, the moon
and the gentle light
For I can see two sides to many layers of you
They would explore their differences, connect
with their passion but respect each other's
spaces

If you were my muse and I, a potter
I'd make you a vase
It would have a handle and triangle edge so that
you can easily change the water
It would be medium in width and tall in height
I'd ask the painter mo to paint it white

On it, there would be three lavender flowers

If you were my muse and I, a florist
I'd carefully pick out
Seven perfect daffodils
Group them
And tie them in brown string

If you were my muse and I, a writer
I'd describe you not literally, metaphorically
If I spoke of your image I would relate it to
nature
If I spoke of your heart I would relate it to fire
And If I spoke of your soul I would relate it to
the moon

If you were my muse,
I'd always be an artist

Paradise

If parallel universes exist
I hope there is one for us
Spending most of our evenings cooking
Or drinking wine and reading books

I hope there is one
That is filled only with time and space
So we can travel across all of it
Just to find our own place

I hope there is another
Where all of your dreams come true
And if I'm ever on the last flight home
I hope I'm flying home to you

I need there to be another universe
Where it all works out in the end
So I can tell myself it was worth it
If in this one, all I do is pretend

Love Letters

Give me a pen and some paper
I'll write you love letters forever
I'll decorate them with flowers
And recall each beautiful moment we ever spent
together

I'll carve a heart into a tree
Our initials I will scratch
I'll use a stick if I must
To write how we're the perfect match

Give me a beach
Where we can walk hand in hand
Watch the sun as it sets
And I'll write our names in the sand

Give me your sketchbook
I'll paint the colours of your favourite skies
I'll spray it with perfume after
And write endless sentences about your eyes

Give me a napkin and a crayon
I'll use it to write, no matter my age
I'll leave my number as if it's the first time
With a kiss at the bottom of the page

Give me your birthday card
I'll always fill it with love
And use cheesy similes
Like how your heart fits mine like a glove

But if there's a world where there are no pens
I'll find a way to make it right
So the writer me can express my love for you
Before going to bed at night

So if I never have my pen
And you never have a page
I'll forever write you love letters
In an endless amount of ways

Philia

I've found another love
One that's written within the stars
One that feels embedded within the universe
One that shouts drunken I love you's across
sticky university bars

She's, suggesting proper cheesy chips
She's, "text me when you're home"
She's, spontaneous beach trips
She's, "I won't let you walk alone"

It's soft and kind
Platonically intimate and warm
It's rare to find
But not completely out of the norm

It's everything you need it to be
Exactly when you need it
It's feeling so open and free
Without needing to deep it

It's so special
No it really is
It's not everyday
You find a love quite like this

It's not the love for a man
Or a sister or a brother
Nor is it the love for your mum or dad
Or a significant other

It's the love you find
In twirls and whirls
It's the love you find
Within you and your girls

www.ingramcontent.com/pod-product-compliance
Lightning Source LLC
LaVergne TN
LVHW051231200726

843510LV00011B/1546